Wounds Of Love !

Dr.Sayyeda Adiba Ahmad

BookLeaf
Publishing

India | USA | UK

Wounds Of Love ! © 2024 Dr.Sayyeda Adiba Ahmad

All rights reserved.

No part of this publication may be reproduced, stored in a retrieval system, or transmitted, in any form or by any means, electronic, mechanical, photocopying, recording or otherwise, without the prior written permission of the presenters.

Dr.Sayyeda Adiba Ahmad asserts the moral right to be identified as the author of this work.

Presentation by *BookLeaf Publishing*

Web: www.bookleafpub.com

E-mail: info@bookleafpub.com

ISBN: 9789363315648

First edition 2024

*This book is dedicated soulfully to the Love of
my life, My half-soul, My Son, MOEZ.*

ACKNOWLEDGEMENT

I couldn't possibly ever have written a book without acknowledging the two most important women in my life, who mean the world to me and have loved me unconditionally. They will forever be my number ones and the source of everything good in me! My beautiful ladies—my mother, Nasim Bano, and my momma (sis-in-law), Shagufta Khanam.

Halo

Wounds of my heart,
never witnessed nor heard....
affectionate smile...
all the love,
desires...
in your arms I rest,
what follows is love....
wandering in the realms of divinity...
infinite,
surreal....
withered within,
that pounding hollow,
Halo of my dreams....

Undeniably Accepted

Undeniably accepted...
Bleeding through my veins,
The compassion, it's insane......
Self-worth, turned over...
Like the world was more sane.....
But far am I to hear, to live, to fear....
No more denials,
No more trials...
Undeniably accepted......
Every breath, introspected.........

Lost

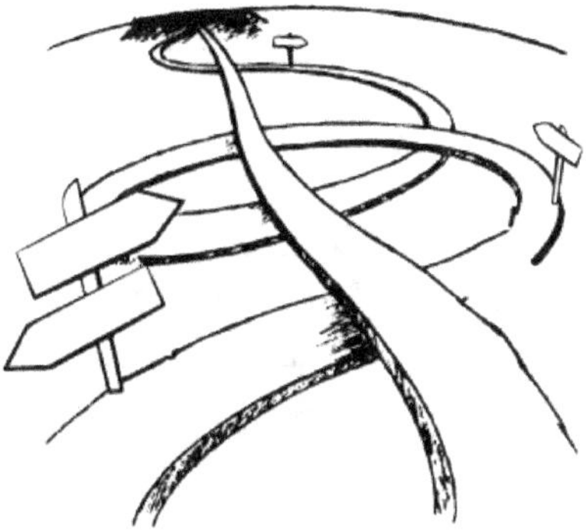

Lost....
What's worth?..
No bliss, unheard.......
Forevers were never mine,
I sing along on the roads divine...
Wherever shall I reach....maybe it's a breach.....
Far-fetched, yet somehow it shines...
I dream and dream to define.....
Perhaps somewhere I belong...
Somewhere shall someday be mine...

Horizons of Sunshine

In the horizons of incapacitating love,
A reminder once came through....
Like the hues of the evening sunset,
The breeze of faint wet soil filled me up with the
essence of everlasting joy....
An essentially soothing note......
Love was bound to be.....
Soaring up high, letting the winds pass by.....
The struggle of life within me seemed like the
pain I was forever yearning to feel.....
Every beat aligned,
A life within mine.....
Not a moment to forget,
Innate desire,
Love was bound to be like no other......
The Horizons of my Sunshine......

Solitude

In solitude I stand....
Chaos, transcending.....
Enlighten me with a world I knew,
Innocent, childlike hue.
Looking across, wherever I could....
Probably shrewd....

Ya Rabb

I seek the light, ya Rabb, I wonder where it is.....
I search the soul, ya Rabb, only to find the
bliss....
I wonder if I am content with this world....
I wonder if what I have is enough....
I seek what is to end....
And maybe when the end is near, I'll seek the
truth....
I search my soul and I search for the light no
more.....

Love?

Love?...
Would you define....
Draw me that line....
In the darkness, you stand at the edge of that
shore......?
With the sunsets, do you hymn your heart out
and more......?
Would you define?
Draw me that line....

Normal

They spoke about beauty,
They spoke about perfection....
All I ever heard was that 'NORMAL' wasn't my impression......
It came from close,
It came from loved ones....
A different approach, in each expression.....
NORMAL was far away.....
It was never the closest I came, even today.....
Such stories I have, so much to say.....
How was I ever wrong? I ask each one, but could I ever say?....
"She's lucky to have that, even when she's like that"

She doesn't deserve love, is that what you
believe to mean or say?
"Mask up! Get beautiful"
Are you that afraid?.....
Yet I have come to accept,
Love wasn't meant to be Hers....
The world has taught, oh! quite so well....
I'll believe what people say....
I still wonder though, what's with the world, I
can never comprehend....
NORMAL has no extinction,
It was never meant to begin with theirs.....

Twirling in the storms

Twirling in the storms of my past.....
Seeking withdrawal from what lasts....
Unending as it seems....
Recapitulates like dreadful dreams.....

Dream

I dream of a life,
Maybe beyond…
Not every song's yours to belong…
Holding my heart, clenched, it's hard…
The pain, is it?
Or insane have I gone?...
Trembling perhaps, my lips, so wrong…
Maybe it's their laugh,
Elated, I go on.
Virtuous? Malicious?
Cling on.
You define, I deny…
My approval's, your wrong.
Elated, I still go on..,
I dream of a life probably beyond….

Defining myself

Defining myself
Come closer you would see, I am no more just a
troll for free.
I stand by, I hear.
I hold more fears…
You curse, you destroy.
In my heart I melt into tears…
Life's easy, life's hard.
Life's always been my rear.
But I stand tall, drenched.
Is there something you ever hear?

Drops of my Heart

The drops that burnt my heart…
Stopped rolling, 've come too far…
I longed for that kiss
Whatever have I missed…
I know not what could be…
Could I be someone's desire, to be His?
If only it was all complete: talks, love, romance,
Is everything I have already missed…
Should life be the same?
Or am I just insane?
I longed for love…. when it never belonged…

I have tried hard

I have tried hard, never felt it would be so…
Frustrated, agitated, I seek remorse…
You'll heal, or so was I told…
You are stuck?!
Well, should I be more clear?...
I never felt that love.
Was I just blind to bear?
Pity, yes I do, myself…
No longer can I hold…
Romance is for the pretty…
Have you ever been told?
Clear enough,
Well I need no more hold…

A Mess

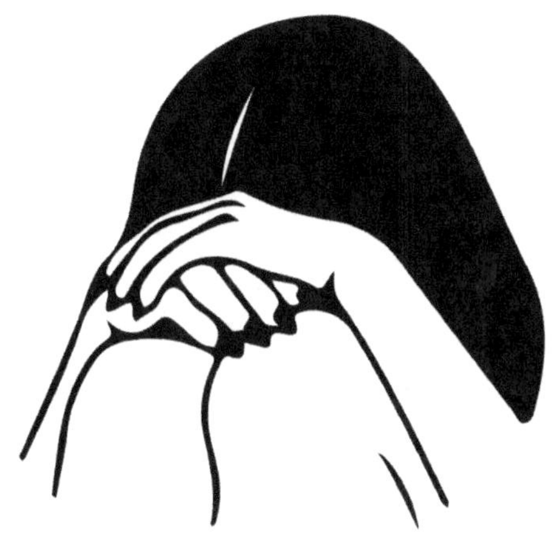

I wanted that "I love you"
I wanted those "I miss you's"
I wanted all that, I still do…
Maybe it's too late to blame you…
I've created a mess,
My own, yes…
I always knew it wasn't who I could ever be...
Wasn't it something I deserved?...
It was all not for me…
LOVE…
Unheard, Solus.

Dreamy Eyes

Those dreamy eyes… the longing…
Holding arms, caressing…
Love between us, that moment, that touch…
Kissed through the night… you just know my
veins, my blush…
I wanted to define, draw you that line…
If only you could feel my longing, my need of
belonging…
The moments have long gone, perhaps lost in an
unheard, forgotten song…
Passing through nights in tears, haven't heard
words of cheers…
Lost control, lost in the space of time…
Love was but not ever mine….

Comprehend

Some people respond… but do not
comprehend…
Sometimes, to fail is important.

Wish

I wish… I only wish that this could be…
The love I have seen was also for me…
Those kisses, those hugs, those playful words…
The laughter, the fun…
That romantic burn…
I only wish I could feel them too…
I wish and I only can wish…

Burning Flames

Burning inside,
Those flames we hide.
Uncanny resemblance…
Swamped.
Inconvenient?
Take a plight, soul's paradise.
Those midnight dreams,
Two realms to breach.
Heaven's… maybe, accolade?

Stairway

A stairway to scale… impatient, do we hail?
Unrest, it's a test.
This voice inside.
Beaming with glee…
However, do we heal?...
Aboard a new life…
A path to infer…
Conquer.

First Kiss

Nobody ever said 'I Love You'
Never meant the words were ever so true....
All I felt was void and vain in my heart....
Let alone sympathy or gratitude....
They say you'll find your love....
Somewhere out there, they'll hold you too...
Someday, maybe in my beautiful, lonely dreams
I'll have my first kiss too....

I Tried

I tried,
I lied,
And one day I denied
Everything....
Lastly,
Curse
Mistake
Hate?
Anger?
Sometimes I ask myself what's worth....
My life?
Or that everyday I die?......

Lover's Patrol

Just a dream, the visuals, the screams.
When love was no more, just a desire…
Those tears hitting through the rains…
Winding up the soul,
Lover's patrol…
Aching heart,
Flowing sorrows,
Betrayal have I known?
Like the end of an ocean, my heart feels
drowned…
Within the saturation of my love, this seems like
an unwanted hound…
Spellbound by eternity, was there ever such a
thing to begin with…?
Whatever have I seen,
A wrenching disaster, so vivid.
Trembling aura, not a whisper to hear…
Lover's patrol, sheer…

Hidden

Faces I have seen
Hidden, unseen
Fire through my veins, burning me insane…
Reckless, unstoppable…
Twisted were the words,
Heartfelt apologies
None revered…
Won't let me cry, won't let me sigh
Shattered soul.
Pieces to assemble, nomadic row.
Faces I have seen
Hidden, Unseen.

www.ingramcontent.com/pod-product-compliance
Lightning Source LLC
LaVergne TN
LVHW021355200726

843509LV00014B/2861